LESTER B. PEARSON

POLITICIAN AND PUBLIC SERVANT WHO GAVE CANADA A NEW FLAG | CANADIAN HISTORY FOR KIDS

True Canadian Heroes

www.ProfessorBeaver.ca

Print Edition: 9780228235507
Digital Edition: 9780228235514
Hardcover Edition: 9780228235989

Published by Speedy Publishing Canada Limited

PROFESSOR
BEAVER
Building Smarter and Brighter Minds

Table of Contents

Quick Facts

LESTER B. PEARSON

Lester Bowles Pearson, who was known to many as Mike, was born in 1897 and died in 1972. There are several reasons why he is a well known Canadian. He served as a soldier, a civil servant (a person who works for a certain department of the government and whose duties include working on behalf of the people in the country), a diplomat and prime minister for the Liberal Party.

DID YOU KNOW?

A diplomat is a person whose job is to represent his/her government overseas. A diplomat is responsible for making sure that relations are good with the government of the foreign country to which s/he is sent.

Lester is probably most remembered nationally for his role in the Canada Pension Plan (CPP), health care, the army and the new Canadian flag. In addition, he made a big impact as a diplomat and he helped to come up with Canada's foreign policy (the official way in which one country has relations with other countries) after the Second World War (WWII).

Internationally, he is probably most remembered for winning a Nobel Peace Prize. He received this prize for his help in contributing to Britain and France (two European countries) leaving Egypt (a country in Northeast Africa).

LESTER IS MOST REMEMBERED FOR WINNING A NOBEL PEACE PRIZE.

DID YOU KNOW?

A Nobel Peace Prize is an award that is given to a person who has done a lot to keep peace in the world. It is given by the Nobel Foundation every year. The Nobel Foundation was started as a result of the last will of Alfred Nobel, the man who invented dynamite.

NOBEL PEACE PRIZE MEDAL

Lester's Childhood and Early Days

Lester B. Pearson was born on April 23, 1897 in Newtonbrook (which is now a part of Toronto) in the province of Ontario.

DID YOU KNOW?

Toronto is the capital city of the province of Ontario. The capital city is the city in which the government offices are located. Toronto is also the largest city in Canada.

NATHAN PHILLIPS SQUARE AND TORONTO SIGN
IN DOWNTOWN TORONTO, ONTARIO, CANADA

AURORA METHODIST CHURCH IN AURORA, ONTARIO

Lester's father's name was Edwin Arthur Pearson and his mother's name was Annie Sarah Pearson. His father was a Methodist Minister. Lester had two brothers, Vaughan and Marmaduke Pearson.

Although Lester was born in Newtonbrook, this is not where he grew up. His father, being a Methodist Minister, relocated (moved) the family to Aurora, Ontario to accept the position as a minister for the Aurora Methodist Church.

Lester spent the early part of his childhood in Aurora and attended school there. He enjoyed playing sports and he played for the Aurora Rugby Team. He also played lacrosse and baseball.

LESTER DURING A BASEBALL GAME DEMONSTRATION.

HAMILTON COLLEGIATE INSTITUTE

Because his father was a Methodist Minister, Lester had to move from one place to another when his father was transferred. When Lester was sixteen years of age, he graduated from Hamilton Collegiate Institute. This institute was in Hamilton, a city on the west side of Lake Ontario.

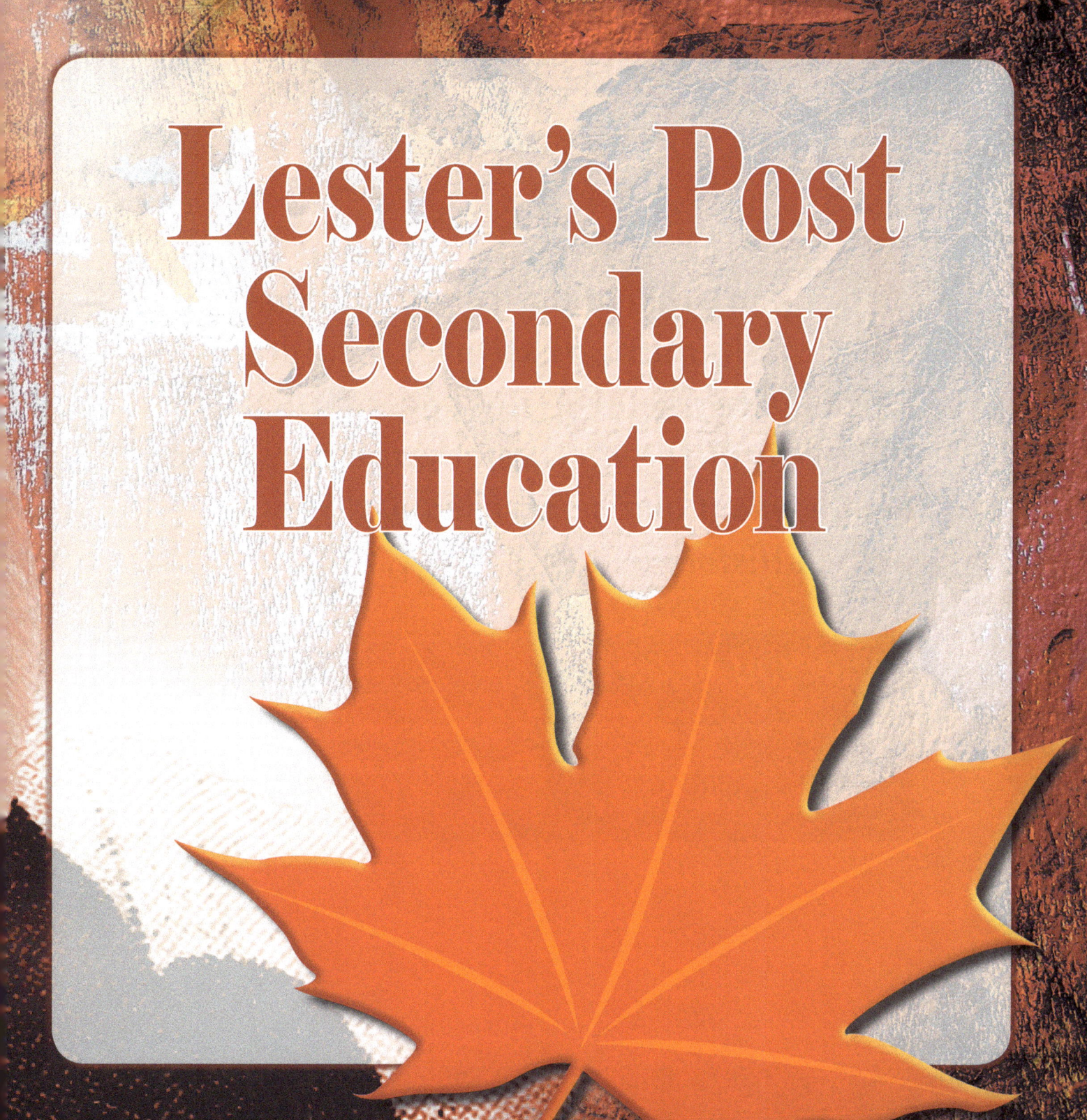

Upon graduating from Hamilton Collegiate Institute, Lester enrolled in Victoria College at the University of Toronto. Lester was a very good student and he excelled (did very well) in History and Psychology.

DID YOU KNOW?

Post-secondary education is the education a person receives after high school, for example at college or university.

PI GAMMA MU HONOUR
SOCIETY PENDANT AND PIN

He did so well that he was admitted into the University of Toronto's chapter (section) of the Pi Gamma Mu Honour Society.

DID YOU KNOW?

The Pi Gamma Mu Honour Society was founded (started) in Kansas in the United States of America (USA), in 1924. It is a society that focuses on doing exceptionally well in the social sciences and puts a lot of importance on scholarship.

Not only was Lester a very good student academically, he was also very good at sports. His athletic abilities did not go unnoticed at the University of Toronto. He played basketball and he continued with rugby, a sport that he had played earlier in his childhood.

LESTER PLAYED RUGBY, A SPORT THAT HE HAD PLAYED EARLIER IN HIS CHILDHOOD.

ST. JOHN'S COLLEGE,
OXFORD UNIVERSITY

Lester's outstanding scholastic achievement did not end at the University of Toronto. He was later offered a scholarship from St. John's College at Oxford University in England, a country in the United Kingdom (U.K.) in Europe. The scholarship was from 1921 to 1923.

Lester travelled to England to attend Oxford University. His studies lasted for a period of two years and he graduated with a Bachelor of Arts (B.A.) in Modern History. He finished with Second-Class Honours. He later received a Master of Arts (M.A.) from Oxford University.

While studying at Oxford University, Lester, once again, shone as an athlete. He spent time playing hockey as a member of the Ice Hockey Club. In 1923, the team for which he played was awarded the very first Spengler Cup.

DID YOU KNOW?

The Spengler Cup is the prize that is given to the winning team from a hockey tournament that occurs annually (every year) in Switzerland, a country in Europe.

OXFORD UNIVERSITY VS. SWITZERLAND HOCKEY GAME. LESTER IS AT RIGHT FRONT, CA. 1922 - 1923.

LESTER TRAVELLED AROUND NORTH AMERICA AS A MEMBER OF THE LACROSSE TEAM.

Not only that, Lester travelled around North America as a member of the Lacrosse team. This team was a joint team of both Oxford University and Cambridge University, two universities in England.

After Oxford, Lester returned to Canada and taught History at the University of Toronto. While teaching there, he also helped in the capacity of coach for the university's hockey and football teams.

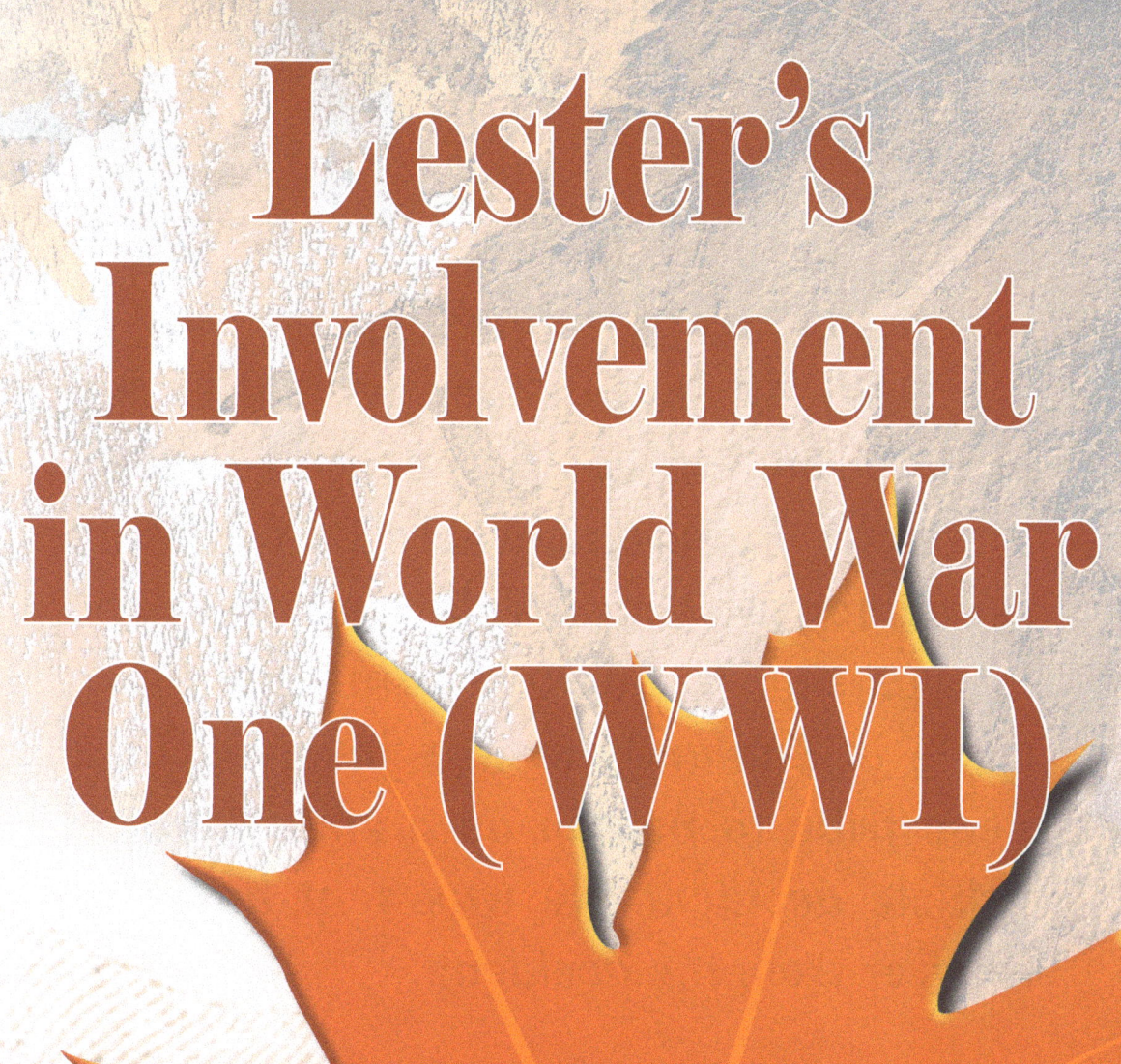

Lester's Involvement in World War One (WWI)

In 1915, Lester signed up for duty in WWI by joining the Medical Corps of the Army. He was first sent to Greece, a country in Europe, where he faithfully served for two years. Following that duty, he was sent to England. Unfortunately, while in England, he was involved in a pedestrian (a person on a street)/motor vehicle accident. He was sent home to recover from the accident.

LESTER SERVED WITH THE CANADIAN ARMY MEDICAL CORPS IN WWI.

Lester's Personal Life

Lester married a former University of Toronto student of his by the name of Maryon Moody. She was from Winnipeg, the capital and largest city of the province of Manitoba. It was 1924 when they got married. Soon after their marriage, they had two children, a son and a daughter.

MARYON MOODY

A few years later, in 1927, Lester decided to have a career change. He took the exam that is required for entrance into the Foreign service (working as a diplomat overseas).

Lester did extremely well on the exam. He soon resigned from his job at the University of Toronto to head for the Department of External Affairs, which is currently (now) known as the Department of Foreign Affairs, Trade and Development.

Lester's Role as a Civil Servant and a Diplomat

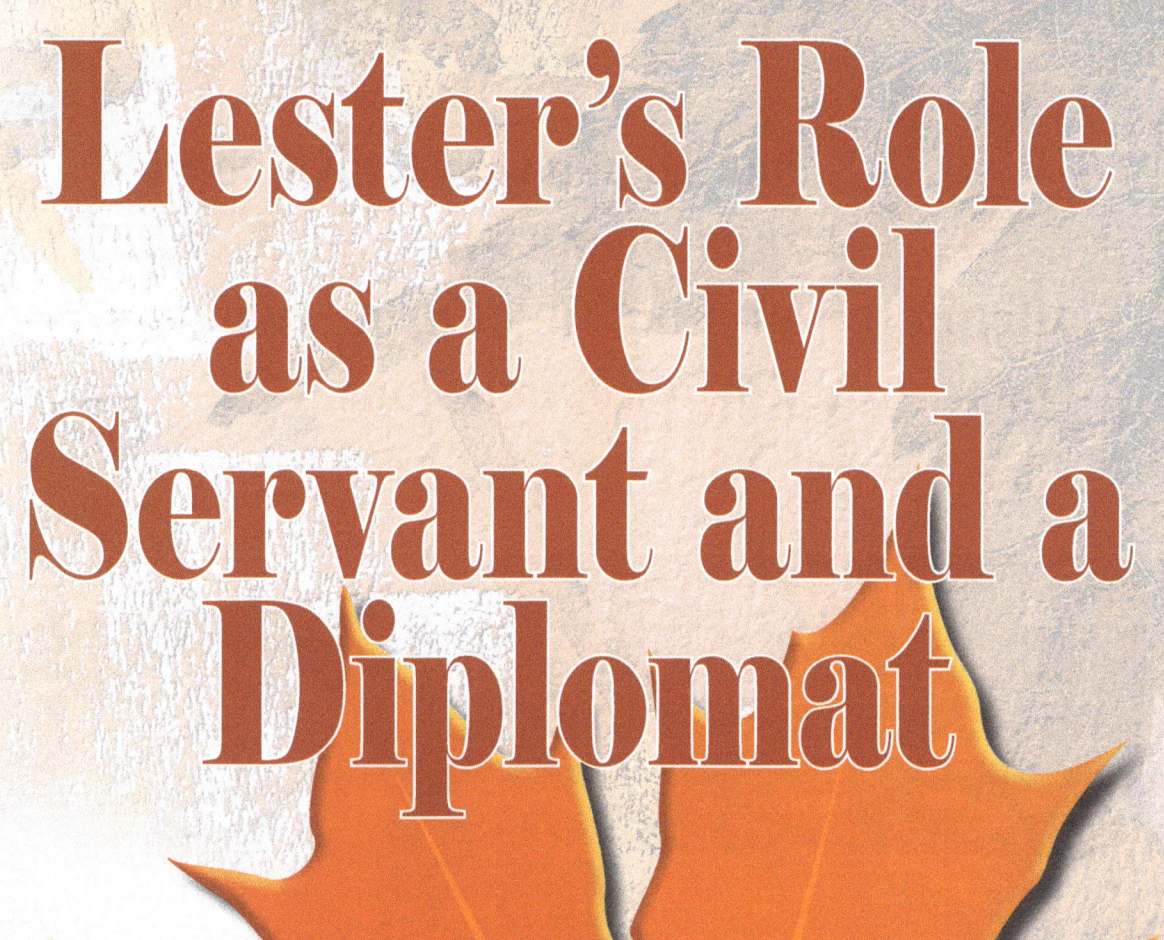

When Lester was a civil service, then Prime Minister Richard Bennett put him in charge two very important Royal Commissions.

48

PRIME MINISTER RICHARD
BEDFORD BENNETT

One Royal Commission was given to Lester in 1931 and it was to find out grain futures (contracts that deal with many important things involved with how grains will be sold and delivered). The other one was handed to him in 1934 and it was to gather information on price spreads choice strategies (methods) that are used in the area of investment (putting money into a business in order to make a profit) and finance (how money is managed). Lester proved himself to be very good at conducting Royal Commissions.

In 1939, Lester was sent overseas to the U.K. to work in the Canadian High Commission.

DID YOU KNOW?

The High Commission of Canada serves the same role as an embassy, the official office of one country's government that is located in a foreign country.

CANADIAN HIGH COMMISSION BUILDING IN TRAFALGAR SQUARE, LONDON, ENGLAND

Lester served in the U.K. at the same time as WWII. He became involved in helping the military to organize non-combative (non-fighting) duties. One responsibility in which Lester made a positive impact was helping refugees (persons who have fled their country because their lives were in danger).

Upon completing his role at the High Commission of Canada to the U.K., he was sent to Ottawa, Ontario, the capital city of Canada.

After that, he was transferred to the Canadian Embassy in Washington, D.C., the capital of the USA, to be a ministerial counsellor (a high-ranking diplomat but not the person who has the lead role). A couple years later, he was given a promotion. He was made the Canadian Ambassador to the USA, a position he filled until the fall of 1946.

DID YOU KNOW?

An ambassador is the highest position held in an embassy. The ambassador's role is to represent his/her country's government and to promote good relations.

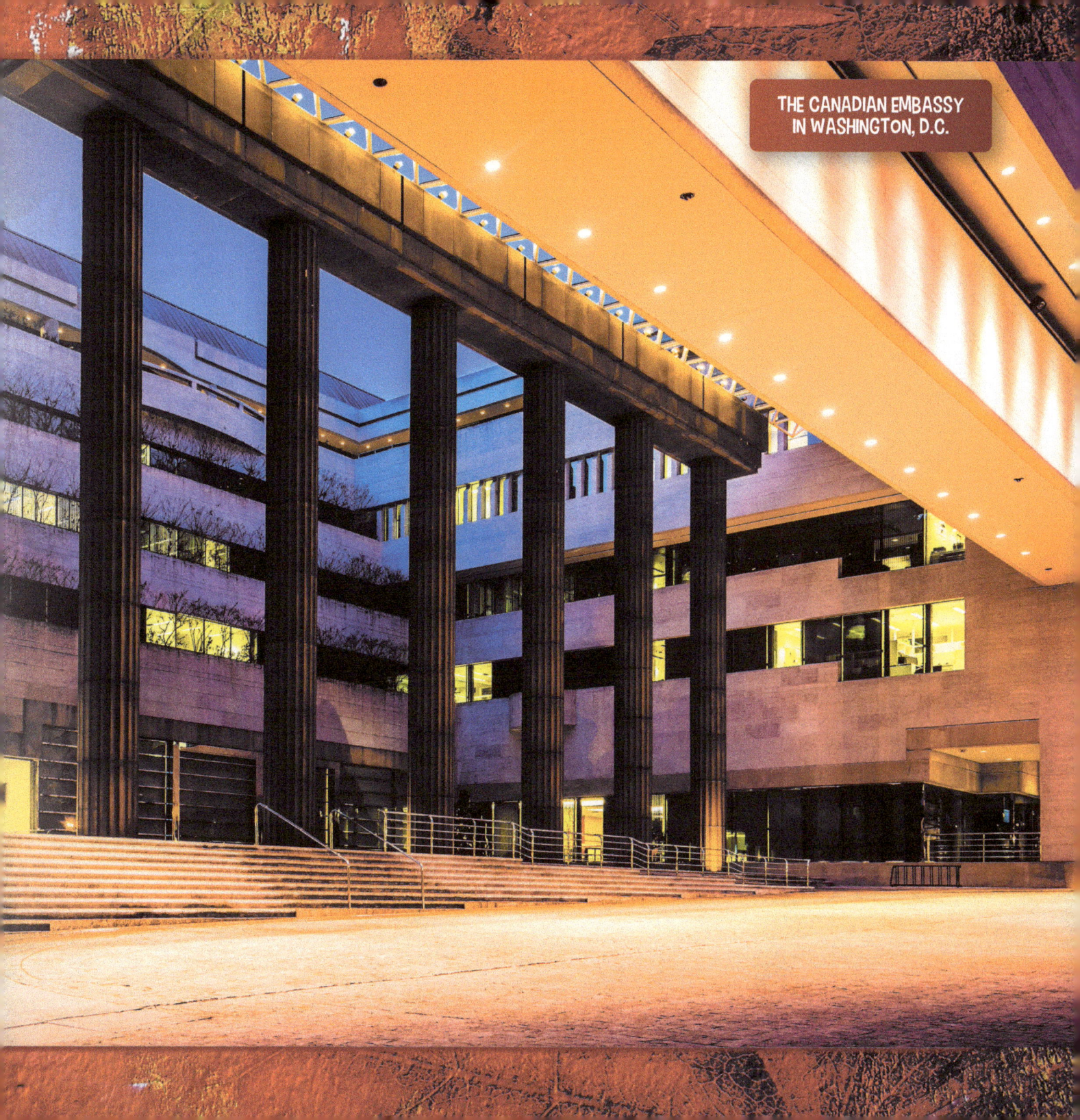

THE CANADIAN EMBASSY
IN WASHINGTON, D.C.

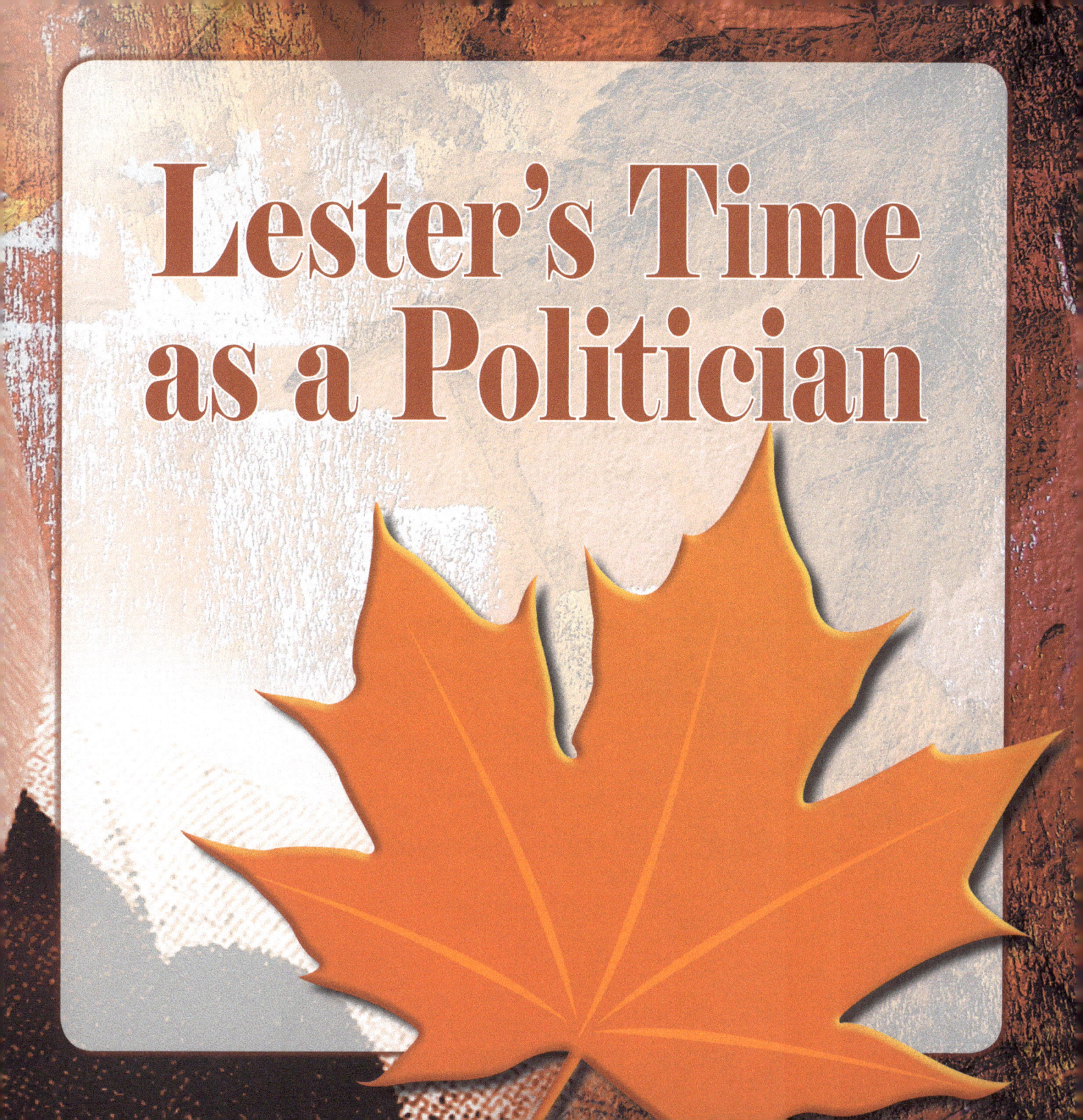

Lester's Time as a Politician

Lester was made a foreign minister in 1948 by the prime minister.

Not long after that, he was elected into the House of Commons for the riding (area) known as Algoma East. It is located in northern Ontario.

THE HOUSE OF COMMONS INSIDE
PARLIAMENT HILL IN OTTAWA

LESTER SENT CANADIANS TO THE KOREAN WAR TO JOIN THE COALITION ARMY OF THE UN.

After this, Lester became the Secretary of State for External Affairs, an office he held for a fairly short period of time. In this role, he sent Canadians to the Korean War to join the coalition (partnership) army of the United Nations (UN), an international organization that tries to promote peace and unity.

His contribution to peace is probably best remembered for the role he played in 1956 in Egypt. This is when UN peacekeepers arrived so that the British and the French could leave Egypt peacefully. In 1957, he received the Nobel Peace Price for his effort in securing a peaceful British and French departure from Egypt.

Following that, in 1958, he was voted in as the Liberal Party leader.

LESTER RECEIVED THE NOBEL PEACE PRICE IN 1957.

Lester became the prime minister of Canada in 1963 and he is remembered for being very successful in the role of prime minister. He helped to make positive contributions to social programs for Canadians. Some examples include health care, CPP and student loans so that students can afford to attend post-secondary institutions.

He was also responsible for bringing about the Royal Commission on Bilingualism (speaking two languages) and Biculturalism (having two cultures). In addition, he oversaw a Royal Commission on the Status of Women.

LESTER BECAME THE PRIME MINISTER OF CANADA IN 1963.

CANADA PROSPERED UNDER LESTER'S LEADERSHIP AND HE MADE SURE CANADIAN INTERESTS WERE UPHELD.

The country of Canada prospered (did well) under Lester's leadership and he made sure that Canadian interests were upheld (kept). This was obvious because there was a low unemployment (not having a job) rate during his time as prime minister. Moreover, he most likely saved a lot of lives by refusing to allow Canada to enter the Vietnam War.

Lester also established an immigration (moving to another country to live and become a citizen) system that was free of discrimination (unfair treatment of a person(s) only because of race, religion, culture, or the like).

The year that Canada became one-hundred years old happened during Lester's time as prime minister. He made sure that Canadians had a chance to celebrate the one hundredth e anniversary. For his role in the festivities, which included the arrival of the Centennial Flame to Parliament Hill, he was called Newsmaker of the Year by The Canadian Press.

CENTENNIAL FLAME ON PARLIAMENT HILL IN OTTAWA, ONTARIO, CANADA

Lester's government is responsible for unifying (bringing together) all of the different types of national defence, such as the Royal Canadian Air Force, the Army, and the Navy. It is now the Canadian Forces and it was established on February 1, 1968.

Lester officially announced that he was going to retire as a politician on December 14, 1967. He stepped down as prime minister in 1968.

CANADIAN ARMED FORCES UNIFORMS FOR WORK USE ON SHIPBOARD, IN FIELD AND AIR OPERATIONS

CANADA

CANADA

Lester's Role after Retiring from Politics

THE WORLD BANK BUILDING HEADQUARTERS ON PENNSYLVANIA AVENUE, WASHINGTON D.C., USA

After his retirement from politics, Lester became the chairperson (head) for the Pearson Commission on International Development.

DID YOU KNOW?

The Pearson Commission on International Development was set up to find out how good the organization of the World Bank's development assistance (help) had been within the two decades (twenty years) before 1968. Lester and his colleagues had to write a report and offer suggestions for future projects.

Lester also became a lecturer at Carleton University in Ottawa. He lectured in Political Science and History. In addition, he held the position of chancellor (leader) of the same university until he passed away.

CARLETON UNIVERSITY IN OTTAWA

He died on December 27, 1972 from cancer at his home in the city of Ottawa. He was seventy-five years of age.

PEARSON

LESTER BOWLES PEARSON
O.B.E., P.C., C.C., O.M.
PRIME MINISTER OF CANADA
PREMIER MINISTRE DU CANADA
1963 – 1968
NOBEL PEACE PRIZE
1957
1897 — 1972
BELOVED HUSBAND OF
MARYON ELSPETH MOODY

PEARSON'S GRAVESTONE
IN WAKEFIELD, QUEBEC

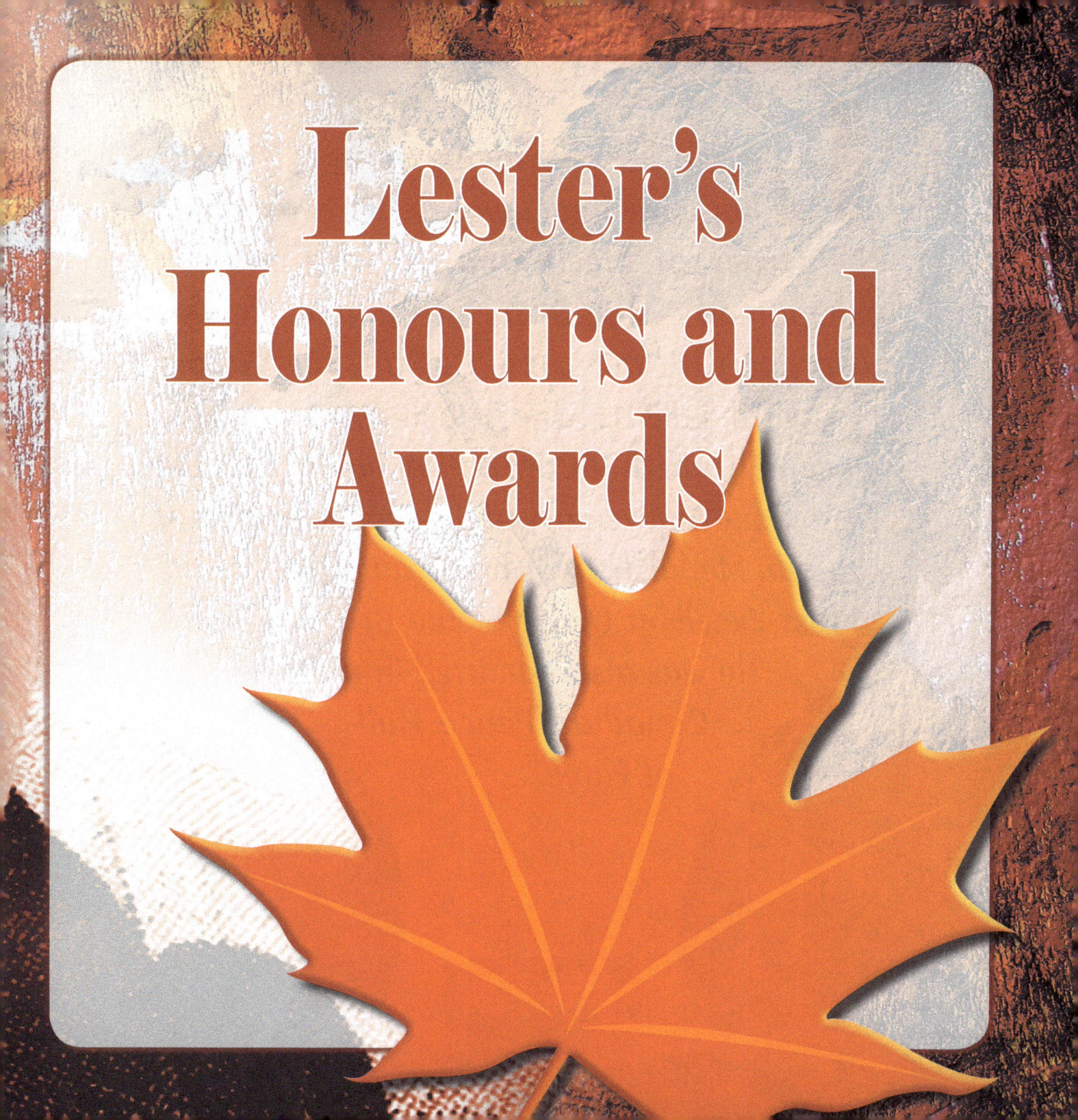

Lester's
Honours and
Awards

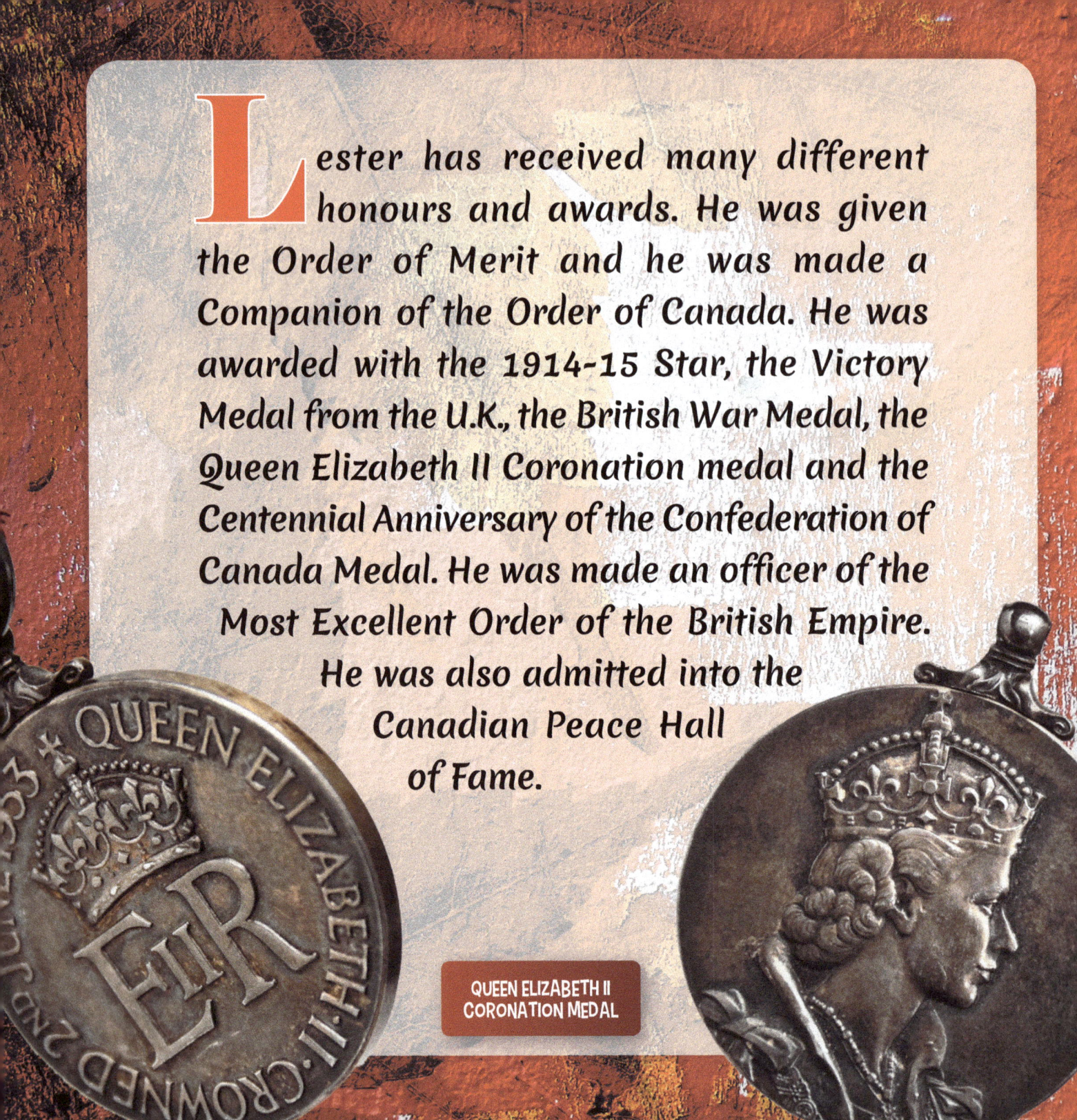

Lester has received many different honours and awards. He was given the Order of Merit and he was made a Companion of the Order of Canada. He was awarded with the 1914-15 Star, the Victory Medal from the U.K., the British War Medal, the Queen Elizabeth II Coronation medal and the Centennial Anniversary of the Confederation of Canada Medal. He was made an officer of the Most Excellent Order of the British Empire. He was also admitted into the Canadian Peace Hall of Fame.

QUEEN ELIZABETH II
CORONATION MEDAL

Many academic institutions have been named after him. Also, some buildings and other structures have been named in his honour. One example is Lester B. Pearson International Airport in Toronto.

LESTER B. PEARSON INTERNATIONAL AIRPORT IN TORONTO

Many universities, both in Canada and abroad, have bestowed (given) honorary degrees to him.

Lester has been honoured for his athletic ability. In addition to receiving an award for hockey, he has been inducted into the Canadian Baseball Hall of Fame as well as the University of Toronto's Sports Hall of Fame.

An award, which is named in honour of him, The Pearson Peace Medal, is presented to somebody every year. This award is given to a person who has done something to promote peace or who has participated in other worthy causes.

Lester B. Pearson can certainly be considered a true Canadian hero.

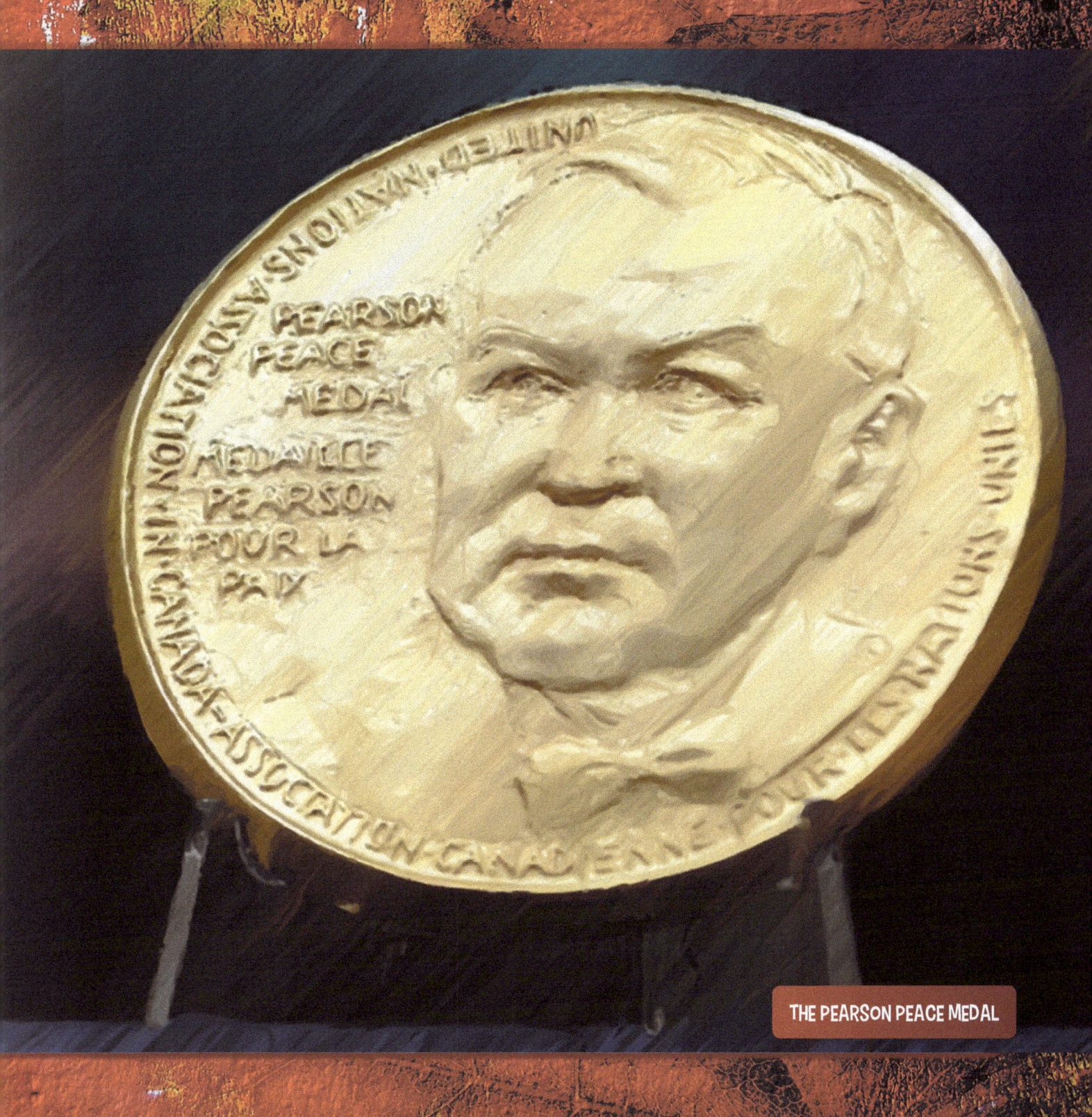

UNITED·NATIONS·ASSOCIATION·IN·CANADA-ASSOCIATION·CANADIENNE·POUR·LES·NATIONS·UNIES

PEARSON
PEACE
MEDAL

MEDAILLE
PEARSON
POUR LA
PAIX

THE PEARSON PEACE MEDAL

Visit

www.truecanadians.ca

to learn about other True Canadian stories and/or view our catalogue of edutaining children's books.

TRUE CANADIAN SERIES

Lightning Source UK Ltd.
Milton Keynes UK
UKHW050752050121
376449UK00002B/86